Lena loved secrets. Secrets about birthday presents, hide-and-seek spots, and whispers with her best friend.
But one day, she had a secret that didn't feel fun.

Lena's friend Jake told her,
"This is our special secret.
You can't tell anyone."
But inside, Lena's tummy
felt tight. This secret felt
different.

At home, Lena didn't feel like playing. She didn't feel like drawing or dancing. The secret sat heavy in her chest, like a big, gray cloud.

At bedtime, Lena snuggled
close to her mom.
"Mama," she whispered,
"are all secrets good?"

Her mom smiled gently. "Some secrets are fun, like surprises. But some secrets should be shared—especially if they make you feel sad or scared."

Lena took a deep breath. "Mama... I have a secret, but it doesn't feel good

Her mother hugged her tight. "I'm so glad you told me, sweetheart. You never have to keep a secret that makes you feel bad."

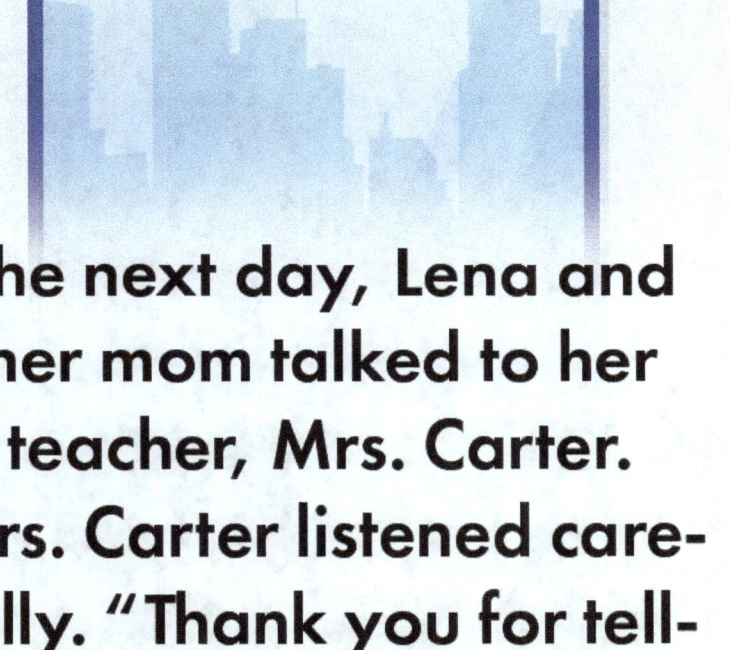

The next day, Lena and her mom talked to her teacher, Mrs. Carter. Mrs. Carter listened carefully. "Thank you for telling me, Lena. You are very brave."

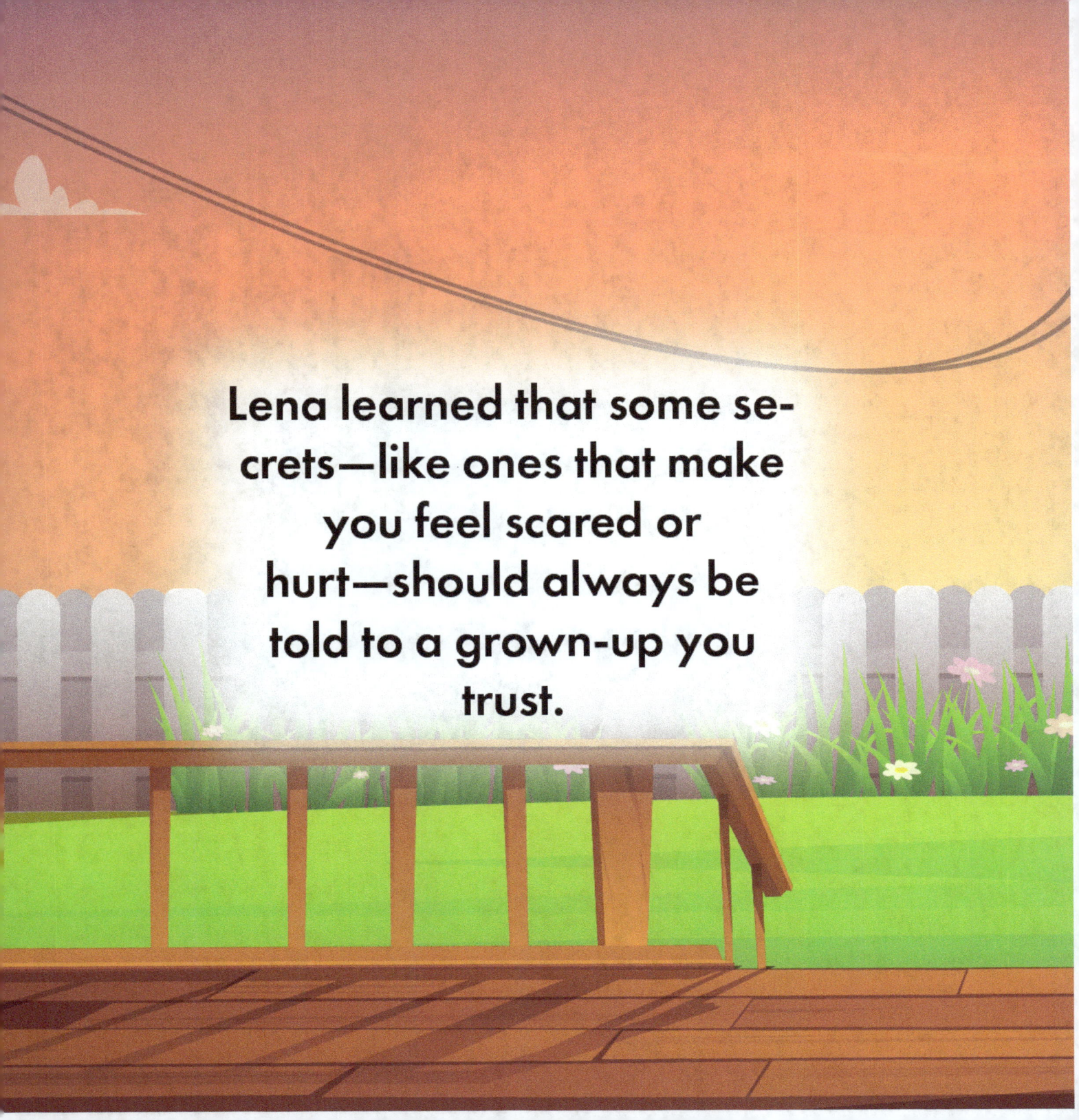

Lena learned that some se-crets—like ones that make you feel scared or hurt—should always be told to a grown-up you trust.

That night, Lena felt lighter, like a bright balloon floating in the sky. She snuggled into bed and smiled. Some secrets should never be kept.

The next day at school, Lena noticed her friend Emma sitting alone, looking sad. Lena sat beside her. "Are you okay?"

Emma hesitated. "I have a secret... but I don't know if I can tell." Lena gently smiled. "You can always tell a grown-up. You don't have to keep it inside."

Lena realized she was
strong and brave.
And now, she could help
others be brave too.

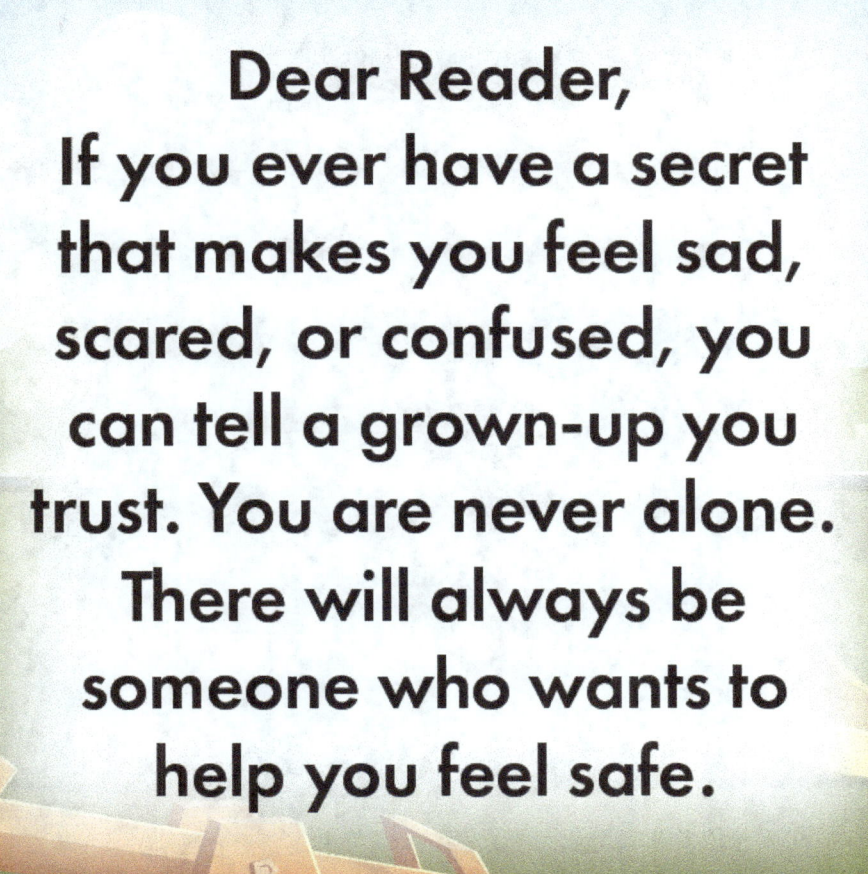

Dear Reader,
If you ever have a secret
that makes you feel sad,
scared, or confused, you
can tell a grown-up you
trust. You are never alone.
There will always be
someone who wants to
help you feel safe.

If you ever feel unsafe or have a secret that makes you uncomfortable, tell someone you trust.
Here are some grown-ups who can help:

- ☑ Parents or guardians
- ☑ Teachers or school counselors
- ☑ Coaches or mentors
- ☑ A family friend or relative you trust

You are never alone. There is always someone who will listen and help.

- It's never your fault if someone asks you to keep a bad secret.
- You don't have to be afraid to tell the truth.
- A trusted grown-up will always want to help keep you safe.
- Keep telling until someone listens!

If you or someone you know needs help, here are safe resources:
- National Child Abuse Hotline: 1-800-4-A-CHILD (1-800-422-4453)
- RAINN (Rape, Abuse & Incest National Network): 1-800-656-HOPE (1-800-656-4673)
- Kids Help Phone: Text CONNECT to 686868 (Canada)

Visit We R Jus Kidz for more resources and information on how to stay safe.

At We R Jus Kidz, we provide education and support to help children and families stay safe.
Want to help?
Visit werjuskidz.org to:
- ☑ Learn more about child safety and prevention
- ☑ Find resources for parents and educators
- ☑ Donate to help us continue our work!

Together, we can make sure that every child feels safe, heard, and protected.